The Fiddlers of Sullivan's Island

by
Jeanie Truesdale Heath

Copyright © 2013 Jeanie Truesdale Heath
All rights reserved.
ISBN #978-0-615-86370-2

Printed in the U.S.A.
Charleston, South Carolina

This book is written in honor of my grandchildren,
Chip and Kellee Ann Cracraft and
Heath, Tanner, and Alec Elizabeth Cleary

IN LOVING MEMORY

My dear friend, Irene Lofton, was a great author and poet. She, too, was a great encourager. She appreciated nature and was married to a man who loved the ocean, gathering oysters, fishing, etc.

One year for Christmas, she and I washed oyster shells, drilled holes in them, put pearls in some, put ribbons through the holes, and decorated our Christmas trees with them. We draped strings of pearls on the tree, and put a large white bow on top. This is only one of many projects we enjoyed doing together.

I think she would be proud to know I wrote this book about the Fiddler Crabs. It would definitely be "her kind of book," and I hope it will be yours, too.

The Fiddlers of Sullivan's Island

MORE REVIEWS FOR

The Fiddlers of Sullivan's Island
by Jeanie Truesdale Heath

"Writer Jeanie Heath can make you sense the grit of the sand between your toes, as you avoid crushing scores of Fiddler Crabs scurrying to find their way from the beach to their homes in the Pluff Mud. Through the eyes of a child, Heath relates the magic and challenges inherent in growing up in the '40s and '50s on Sullivan's Island, South Carolina, the magnetic, but largely obscure slice of land separated from bustling, historic Charleston by a short, but exceedingly necessary, bridge spanning the Intracoastal Waterway. The Island that Jeanie Heath's world consisted of was quite different from the Island we know today. Her mesmerizing descriptions of the various types of shimmering seashells, and species of lush flora and fauna are interwoven with some of her own experiences; thus, providing an entertaining, yet also informative, read. Because that Sullivan's Island exists no more, this little book is a keeper for generations to come."

    Dottie Ashley, *Newspaper Writer*
        Winner of the 2003 Elizabeth Verner Award for excellence in
        coverage of the arts scene in South Carolina

"Jeanie Truesdale Heath captures the spirit of a true Islander whose 'salt runs deep in her veins.' Her imaginative, fascinating tale of Scurry, the Fiddler Crab of Sullivan's Island, proves to be informative and educational, as well as entertaining. A must read for young and old alike. I will be sharing with the young in the classroom."

    Tuffy McInerny Atkins, *Lifelong Islander and Teacher*

TABLE OF CONTENTS

Introduction 1

Chapter 1: What is a Fiddler Crab, Anyway? 5

Chapter 2: Life At Its Best 11

Chapter 3: What's Going On? 17

Chapter 4: Finally, We Can Relax 25

Chapter 5: We Think They're Here to Stay 29

Chapter 6: Our Connection 33

The Fiddlers of Sullivan's Island

This book is dedicated to Hal Coste, a long-time resident of Sullivan's Island, South Carolina, and a true Island Fiddler, with his feet planted deep in the pluff mud.

I met Hal the summer of 2012, when he heard I was writing a book about the Island. He invited me to his house to look at his collection of old pictures and other special memorabilia he has collected over the years, including items deemed useless. He uses his talents by giving these items new life and artistic substance. His profession is restoring historic houses and buildings.

He offered to drive me around in his cart to show me how the Island has changed. During the course of conversation, I told him I had a new bucket seat that I wanted to hang from the ceiling on my screen porch.

I hardly got the words out my mouth when we were on the way to my house in Mount Pleasant. It was about 3:00 pm. He immediately got busy. He located a strong beam, hung the swing for me, built a frame to keep it stationary, and the job was completed by dark. He insisted on not being paid.

While he was working, I thought, "Hal is scurrying around just like the Fiddler Crabs." They are true survivors, so is he. They enjoy scurrying around, so does he. They help protect the wetlands and environment without getting anything in return ... just as Hal helped me, without getting anything in return."

Many thanks to you, Hal, from one Fiddler to another.

~ *Jeanie Truesdale Heath*

A Fiddle Riddle

Is it an instrument?

Is it a crab?

Is it a person?

Is it all 3?

Read on to find out!

The Fiddlers of Sullivan's Island

Enter the fascinating world of the Fiddler Crab ...

The Fiddlers of Sullivan's Island

I am a Fiddler Crab named Scurry.

I got that name because I can run really fast and scurry all around in the marsh and on the beach. You have to be really fast to catch me or any other Fiddler Crab before we burrow into our homes in the ground.

Books have been written about our friends like the Horseshoe Crab, the turtle, and the Alligator who live close by.

Introduction

Once upon a time,

Fiddler Crabs like me, roamed freely on an Island known as Sullivan's.

It is a barrier island located off the coast of South Carolina, across the Harbor from the historic port of Charleston.

We had no worries, and we had no cares. Life was good for a long, long time.

Then "something" happened ... something that forever changed life as all Fiddler Crabs knew it.

SULLIVAN'S ISLAND

We decided it was time people learned about us. I was chosen to tell you, because a true Fiddler can tell the story best. Besides, I believe living on this beautiful Sullivan's Island is as good as life gets... even after that "something" altered it.

Male Fiddler Crab

Female Fiddler Crab

Chapter 1
What is a Fiddler Crab, Anyway?

I'm scurrying too fast ... let me start at the beginning.

All we knew was that good ole' Sullivan's Island was a haven for Fiddler Crabs. Whoever gave us the name Fiddler Crab was pretty clever.

The male Fiddler has one large claw and one small. He eats with the small claw by moving it from his mouth to the ground. The large claw goes up in the air and moves up and down while he feeds. It looks as if he is playing the musical instrument called a "fiddle."

The female has two small claws. That's how she can be identified. Fiddler's claws come in really handy for talking, eating, digging, fighting, and playing.

Like all creatures, we need some place to live. We build our homes in shady spots below the surface of the Pluff Mud.

Some of our homes are almost 2 feet deep. When necessary, we can quickly burrow in a hole where we are very safe.

We can stay inside as long as we want, sleep as long as we want, and eat as much as we want.

Things can't get much better than that!

We stay in our homes in the ground during the winter months and come back out in the Spring.

Spring is the time to add to our families and make little baby fiddlers. The male fiddler holds up his largest claw, waves, and sends special noises to get the attention of the females. When the special one is chosen, they go down into his home in the ground where the mating takes place.

The female remains in his home in the ground for two weeks before coming out. When she comes out, she carries her eggs in a sac on her body. The eggs get swept into the water where they float away.

When the time is right and they are fully developed, the hatched eggs come rushing in with the tide.

They begin life in the marsh with the other Fiddler Crabs.

Fiddlers only live about two years. But we are very happy and enjoy the time we have.

One special thing we do is shed our shells as we grow. Sometimes we may lose a claw, but it's not a problem. We just grow another one.

What is really cool is if we lose our larger fiddler claw, we grow a new one on the other side. We learned a long time ago that we need to be really careful when we shed our shell.

The new shell is very soft, and we can get hurt quite easily. So we hide out in our home in the ground until we feel safe to come out again.

Years later we learned that our burrowing through the marsh does something wonderful for everyone: It sifts air through the mud, which helps to add air, and, in turn, helps preserve the wetlands and the environment.

Even though we grow to only 2" long and are small, we are mighty and do mighty important things.

2" Long Maximum

Chapter 1: What is a Fiddler Crab, Anyway?

Chapter 2
Life At Its Best

We are lucky to have the safest places to run and play all day long if we want. We have sword fights, but we only occasionally hurt one another.

Because we can run fast, really fast, we often have races with those strange looking sand crabs, or Ghost Crabs, as some folks call them. They are the color of beach sand and blend in nicely with the environment. They can be lots of fun.

Sand crabs are more like us than any other creature that lives on the beach. They, too, live in holes in the ground. However, they do not like the marsh. They love the sandy part of the beach, so that's where their homes are.

There are other creatures that live on the Island: wild horses and hogs, deer, raccoons, rabbits, possums, and birds ... lots of birds. It is nice having them all as neighbors. They do their thing, and we do ours.

They race around the Island, duck around trees, and enjoy the freedom of having nothing that interferes with them. They pretty much ignore us. They learned that even though they can run fast, we can run faster and burrow in the ground before they can blink an eye.

Chapter 2: Life At Its Best

The only ones who sometimes bother us are the blue crabs. So we do our best not to aggravate them.

There is plenty of room for all of us on our beautiful Island with its flowers and trees of all sizes and shapes.

All in all, we enjoy exploring the Island and observing the other sea animals that come to visit.

Once in a while, a storm with lots of rain and very strong winds comes and picks up lots of marsh grass from the marsh. It sweeps it all the way around the end of the Island and piles it up near the sand dunes. It carries a lot of us with it.

We later learned this strong wind is called a North-easterner. We do our best to survive until we can work our way back to our homes in the marsh.

We feel sorry for the jelly fish and others who wash up on the shore when the winds bring the ocean tides close to the sand dunes. Some are not able to make their way back into the water and soon die.

Thank goodness we know how to protect ourselves so it won't happen to us.

Little did we know how valuable knowing how to survive Mother Nature and getting along with other creatures would prove to be.

Chapter 2: Life At Its Best

Chapter 3
What's Going On?

WHOA!! Wait a minute!! What was that? Suddenly all the Fiddler Crabs up and down the Island trembled and scattered.

We hurried to our hiding places as fast as we could. Our claws, shivering and clacking, could be heard for miles around.

Our neighbors on a nearby Island also sought shelter in their hiding places.

What was going on?

SLAM!! Plunk!!! Bam!!! Massive creatures appeared, the likes of which we Fiddlers had never seen before. They walked slowly, stalking our Barrier Island, looking everywhere to see if there were anything to fear. Yet they were the ones spreading fear with each huge footprint they left in the sand. The Invaders, as we named them, slowly covered the entire Island, destroying all obstacles in their way.

We stayed in our homes safely hidden below the ground, paralyzed with fright. We silently kept asking one another, "What is going on?" as the ground shook with each step they took.

Deep down we knew their steps were leading us on a journey of discovery that would be life changing for us. Neither we nor our Island paradise would ever be the same again. "But could it still be good, even if it were different?" we wondered.

After waiting a while, we slowly began crawling out of our holes: big claw followed by the smaller claw. Then our eyes peeked out just above the ground. Gingerly we lifted our bodies, taking tiny steps, one feeler at a time.

Next we paused, without moving anything. We looked all around. Finally some of us began rubbing our claws together. Our signals passed all the way across the Island, warning our relatives and friends to be careful and watchful of these Invaders.

These creatures were humongous. They towered over us. They cast huge, dark shadows that were even way bigger than they were. We all huddled close to our hiding places, ready to retreat if one came near us. Gradually we gained courage to come out of hiding. But we stayed close by our place in the marsh, in case we needed to quickly escape their treacherous footprints.

We watched as they cut down trees and dug holes big enough to sit in. Then they pushed what they made down to the creek, shoved it into the water, and jumped in. They began pulling shells from the sides of the marsh and hauling them back to the beach. We watched with interest as they broke open the shells and devoured the meat inside.

We later learned what they ate was called oysters. It was very scary. Were they going to destroy our most favorite place on the entire Island? This land was our land. Even worse, were they going to eat us? What was going to happen?

After they finished eating, they loaded the empty shells back onto the tree with a hole in it, took them back down to the creek, and placed them with the other oysters. They would leave them alone for a while. We soon noticed the beds of shells were getting bigger instead of disappearing.

We breathed a sigh of relief when we finally realized they were not destroying our special homes in the marsh and pluff mud after all. They were actually helping protect it.

The Invaders did other things that amazed us. We watched with increased fascination as they gathered stacks of marsh grass that washed up on the beach from the ocean. They would spread them out to dry and stack them in a pile near the sand dunes.

We stayed really still while they gathered pieces of wood and trimmed them to just the right shape. We stared as they began rubbing them together. Pretty soon smoke began to rise and they carefully placed some weeds they had gathered and piled the marsh grass on top and POOF!! The marsh grass burst into something that was hotter than the sun. We would learn later, it was called "fire." We watched as its massive flames and mountains of smoke rolled towards the sky.

The fire would be used to keep them warm and cook the food they wanted to eat. We soon realized we would not be on their menu. Our tiny size came in handy and explained why others were chosen. We just don't have a whole lot of meat on us. Although we were deeply saddened to see so many others, like blue crab, deer, and hog serve their purpose, it was fascinating to see what the Invaders did with them.

They took long sharp sticks, put them through their catch, and held them over the fire. It took a much bigger stick and a much longer time to cook the animals from the wild. Somehow they knew exactly how long to hold them over the flame and cook them perfectly. They had fun doing it. We watched as their eyes lit up and heard them smack their lips as they devoured these creatures.

They stayed up late, talking and laughing, and having a good ole' time.

As we watched and listened, we came to understand things other living creatures needed to do in order to survive. In fact, we wanted to share what they were doing. We wanted to eat some of these nourishing creatures, too. We would wait out of sight, hoping the Invaders would drop something for our dinner. Fortunately even the trimmings they discarded were a real delicacy for us.

There wasn't too much, however. These Invaders were a clever lot. They used beach sand and other items to make something to hold as well as cook their delicious food.

Chapter 4
Finally, We Can Relax

As time went on, we became increasingly bold, knowing we were too small to be their dinner.

These big Invaders, who liked to be called "humans," were not interested in us. But it turns out we were not ignored after all.

It was their little ones, who they called "children" who discovered we were fun to play with.

They would tie a string around our claw and swing us around until we were so dizzy we could hardly crawl. Sometimes they would walk us down the beach, holding onto the string. But it was okay.

They liked us. We made them laugh. When they held us in their hands, our feelers tickled them. Then they would drop us and off we went, scurrying quickly and burrowing in the mud.

More time passed. It looked as if humans were here to stay. In fact, they were literally putting down roots. They began planting seeds of corn, tomatoes, beans, and other things they called "vegetables" and "fruits." The most fascinating were these great big, huge, green things. They called them "watermelons." They looked really heavy. When the time was right, they would pull one off their green stem, drop it on a log, and break it open.

Boy, did they enjoy eating them.

Inside they were a bright pink color with lots of small black things they called "seeds." They were so excited to eat, they didn't stop to think about the mess they made. They simply had fun. The juice would run down their elbows and get all over their clothes. But that didn't bother them.

The children discovered early on that the black things were not tasty. So they decided to have fun with them.

They had contests to see who could spit them the farthest. They started by drawing a line in the sand, one pretty close to where they stood. As they took turns, they drew the line further and further away, until no one could spit far enough to go beyond it. One human was finally declared the winner. This activity would keep them entertained for hours and hours.

When they finished eating, they would jump in the ocean and swim a while. When they came out of the water, they were somewhat clean and ready to run and play some more. In their own ways, the lives of these humans were beginning to look as wonderful as ours.

Every living creature was finding joy and happiness living on our wonderful Sullivan's Island.

Chapter 5
We Think They're Here to Stay

As they settled in, the humans started building places to sleep at night and protect themselves from bad weather. They were taking space on our Island and making it theirs. There were a few times we thought we might not survive. We feared they'd like the areas near the marsh where we lived. We breathed a big sigh of relief when we realized they didn't. The shelters they were building could not stand strong in the pluff mud like ours did.

BLANCHARD HOUSE
10/15/03 C TIMMONS

The more we came to know the humans, the more we had to admit life was more exciting with them around. We started learning even more new things, which is always good. We slowly began to relax. We even began to trust them.

We finally accepted the fact they would probably never go away. After all, who would ever want to leave a place as heavenly as Sullivan's Island? The secret of our wondrous home was discovered. We would be selfish if we didn't share it with others who respected and loved it, too.

We decided there could and should be enough room for all of us, despite our differences. Humans might have been bigger in size, but we were as big in determination.

My fellow Fiddler Crabs made a pact we have passed down from generation to generation: We would never be overtaken by anyone or anything. We would stick together through thick and thin, beach sand and salt water, pluff mud and marsh grass.

Chapter 5: We Think They're Here to Stay

Pluff (Plough) Mud

A term used to describe the aromatic, gooey tidal mud in the Lowcountry.

Fiddler crabs run all over it ...

Humans walk in it, sink deeper, and often lose their shoes.

The Fiddlers of Sullivan's Island

Chapter 6
Our Connection

Ironically, the pluff mud itself connected us to those invading humans. Of course, we had different ways of dealing with it. But that is what made life so interesting.

Fiddler crabs need the mud of the marsh to build our homes, nestle down, and forget our cares. Humans need to build their homes away from it. Fiddler crabs run all over it, never getting stuck or dirty. They have fun doing it. Humans walk in it, sink deeper, and often lose their shoes. They'd get filthy dirty and angry trying to figure out how they got themselves into such a fix. Eventually they would get free and find their way to solid ground.

For both it is the pluff mud that grounds true Fiddlers. We are all planted in it. Whether we are the crab or human species, it is the very foundation for all living creatures on Sullivan's Island. It nourishes our souls, lifts our spirits, and brings tranquility to our world. Most of all, it forms the confidence that we Fiddlers can face anything and succeed.

Even though Fiddler Crabs are very different from those we first called "Invaders," the love we shared for our Island brought us together. In fact, we eventually shared our first name, Fiddler, with those humans who are born and raised here on Sullivan's Island.

Oh, I am sure they are sometimes crabby...but they are Fiddlers. Even if they go scurrying and find some other place to live, they never forget the fragrance of the pluff mud and the place from which it came. We are joined in a way no one else can truly understand.

It has been hundreds of years since the Fiddler Crab vowed to prevent any creature or anything else on the face of this earth from destroying our claim to the life we learned to love on this exceptional island. We had to work hard to preserve our Island for generations to come.

We succeeded. We still have our space and our rights. Our legacy lives on better than ever because we embraced change and welcomed Invaders now known as "friends."

Chapter 6: Our Connection

Other such friends soon followed the initial invasion. Sullivan's Island has become a haven for humans from countries around the world. Even if they don't actually settle here, they love to visit our beautiful shore to enjoy the benefits of life near the ocean ~ the diverse beauty of the marsh and ocean, the birds, crabs and other wildlife, the feel of the sand and water, and breathing in the uplifting fragrance of the pluff mud.

The Answer to the Fiddle Riddle is now as Plain as Plain can be:

Is it an Instrument, a Crab or a Person?

On Beautiful Sullivan's Island, it is All 3!

Now you come see us real soon, ya' hear?

xxxooo

Scurry

(AKA, Jeanie Truesdale Heath)

Chapter 6: Our Connection

ACKNOWLEDGEMENTS

It is with heartfelt appreciation that I express my gratitude to Archie Burkel, Top Hat for the Hat Ladies of Charleston and author of "Writing Your Memoir," plus more accomplishments than I have room to mention.

I met Archie in 2001 when the Hat Ladies Organization was just getting started. Soon after joining, I took her writing course: "Thou Shalt......11: Honor Your Memory" (a list of ten ways to relax and enjoy writing). Her approach took away all stress and concern about my needing to "have everything perfect." It lists the ten things (using the format for the Ten Commandments) we need to do in order to get our thoughts on paper. Two examples include, #1: Ignore your high school teacher and #4: Strive for progress, not perfection. This was very freeing and inspired me to begin a journey that had been building in my soul for many years. Thanks also, Archie, for doing such a great job of editing the book for me.

I am deeply indebted to Bonny Luthy, owner of Office Express, Inc., for doing such a fantastic job with the design and layout of the book and Chris Luthy for help with the photos. They also recommended two very special people: Becky Moseley, who shared an array of pictures taken on Sullivan's Island - some while lying on "her belly" in the Pluff Mud; and Murray Michaels, who so generously gave his time in helping me with some very important and difficult business issues, which I could not have done without his help and without spending a lot of money. Each of you was "OVER THE TOP" in helping me.

When I decided to illustrate the stories in the book with actual pictures taken on Sullivan's Island, I thought it would be fun to reenact the stories about the ways the Fiddler Crabs entertained us when we were children. I immediately thought about Talia Holliday and knew she would do a great job helping to make the book come alive. Talia is a 2013 kindergarten student who enjoys acting, dancing and singing.

To those friends, Pat Hood Miller, Helena Moore Bradford and Tom Cassem who willingly shared their special gifts, helped reenact scenes and take pictures. Thank you for your interest and support.

"A picture is worth a thousand words." Thanks to Clyde Timmons for sharing his drawing of the Blanchard home, the oldest on Sullivan's Island (early 1800s), to Mary Blanchard for allowing me to use the picture, to Roy Williams, author of The Images of America, Sullivan's Island, for sharing the picture of my family's home on Sullivan's Island, early 1900s, compliments of The South Carolina Archives in Columbia, and to Tuffy McInerny Atkins for allowing me to use a picture of her house, built in the early 2000s.

A big thank you to John Albrecht, a local Charleston artist. He created the book cover as a 16"x20" oil painting on canvas. John is the son of Tommy Albrecht and Helen Tapio Albrecht. John is a juried artist at the Charleston Artist Guild Gallery in Charleston, and currently serves on the Board as Vice President. To view this print and other works by John, please visit his website at www.1-john-albrecht.fineartamerica.com.

Last but not least, many thanks to my cousin, Linda Altman Nettles and my brother, Jerry Truesdale for helping to refresh my memory, and to all my friends for encouraging me to "keep on, keeping on."

As I look back over the year it took me to get this book completed,
I am in awe at the way God worked to help everything come together.
The people, the ideas, the props, the timing, all came together because of
His guidance and help in getting this book written.

The Fiddlers of Sullivan's Island

ABOUT THE AUTHOR

Eugenia Truesdale Heath, better known as Jeanie, grew up on Sullivan's Island, South Carolina in the 1940s-50s. People who were raised on the Island were called "Fiddlers," after the Fiddler Crab.

At a young age, Jeanie connected with the aroma of the Plough Mud in a very special way. She remembers riding across the causeway in their car with no air conditioning, the windows down, and being mesmerized by the smell of the mud. Something would rise up inside her that made her feel she could do anything she wanted. She wished she could put some mud in a jar to get her fix when she needed it. It was and remains very uplifting.

Similarly, Jeanie was intrigued with the Fiddler Crab. She loved the way they walked sideways and the way they scurried into the ground, making it difficult to catch one.

Jeanie is writing her Memoirs which include stories of her growing up as a "Fiddler" on Sullivan's Island, as well as stories shared by others. The book will have a chapter dedicated to Afro-Americans with stories shared about what it was like for them growing up on The Island. One gentleman remembers his Mama telling him, "Son, no matter what, you always remember if anyone asks, you tell them, 'You is a Fiddler.' Once a Fiddler, always a Fiddler."

In addition to being a housewife and mother, Jeanie's love for children encouraged her to start her own Kindergarten. She later became Director of Kinder Care Learning Centers in Mount Pleasant and then District Manager for Charleston and Savannah. Jeanie and her husband, Alec, also owned Heath Farms Produce Market and Bakery on Coleman Boulevard in Mount Pleasant.

The Fiddlers of Sullivan's Island

www.ingramcontent.com/pod-product-compliance
Lightning Source LLC
LaVergne TN
LVHW072126070426
835512LV00002B/25